CW00385335

THE LETTERS OF PELAGIUS

THE LETTERS OF PELAGIUS

CELTIC SOUL FRIEND

Edited by
Robert Van de Weyer

EVESHAM

Arthur James Ltd

Published in 1995 by Arthur James Ltd.
4 Broadway Road, Evesham, Worcestershire, WR11 6BH

ISBN 0-85305-335-9

Typeset by Little Gidding Books in Bembo.
Printed and bound in Great Britain by Biddles Ltd, Guildford.

PREFACE

The original community at Little Gidding was founded in 1626 by Nicholas Ferrar; their beautiful chapel continues to attract numerous visitors. A new community formed in the late 1970s; and, like its predecessor, it includes families and single people, following a simple rule and pattern of prayer.

Little Gidding Books is the publishing arm of the community. In addition to its Prayer Book it publishes each quarter a book of daily readings, and each year a set of readings and meditations for the festival weeks and Lent. These sets of readings may be used in conjunction with the Prayer Book, or on their own. They are supplied directly to Friends of Little Gidding, and are also available to the wider public through bookshops.

The community is dedicated to Christ the Sower; hence its symbol is a cross made from ears of corn. The hand in which 'Little Gidding Books' is written on the cover is that of Nicholas Ferrar – the words have been taken from his letters.

If you would like to have more information, please write to:

The Community of Christ the Sower
Little Gidding
Huntingdon
PE17 5RJ
United Kingdom

INTRODUCTION

Pope Gregory sent his mission to Britain in 597 not to bring Christianity to a heathen people – the Christian faith was already spreading rapidly across the British Isles – but to bring the British church under papal authority; and this involved rooting out the 'Pelagian' heresy. But although the church in Britain eventually embraced Rome, the ideas of Pelagius remained popular. Indeed, as the first major theologian which Britain had produced, he provided the intellectual and moral framework in which Christianity flourished in Britain during the Celtic period. And to this day people in Britain – in the words of the German theologian Karl Barth – remain 'incurably Pelagian'.

Pelagius was born in Britain some time in the mid fourth century, when the country was still under Roman rule. A few decades earlier in 312 Christianity had become, under Emperor Constantine, the official religion of the empire; and as a result bishops and priests rapidly began to acquire great wealth and power. Pelagius like many others was appalled by this development, believing that a disciple of Christ, especially a church leader, should imitate his poverty and humility. Around the year 385 Pelagius travelled to Rome, where he was soon admired for his holiness and for the clarity of his teaching. He became spiritual counsellor to a number of aristocratic men and women who wanted to adopt a simpler and more austere way of life; and he wrote tracts which enjoyed a wide circulation. As one follower wrote: 'I used to regard myself as a worshipper of God; but now for the first time I know how to become a true Christian.'

Pelagius constantly emphasized human freedom. He taught that human emotions and desires are in themselves neither good nor bad, but that human beings can choose whether to direct their emotions and desires to good purposes or bad. In exercising this freedom a person has three sources of guidance: the teaching of Christ, who uniquely directed all his emotions and desires towards goodness; conscience, which is an innate capacity to distinguish good from evil; and prayer, through which God directs and strengthens the human will. Pelagius also stressed the sanctity of all God's creation. He regarded the beauty of nature as a reflection of God's beauty, and he urged people to care for animals and even plants for their own sake.

These simple doctrines provoked the wrath of Augustine, the dominant Christian theologian of the time – and arguably of all time. He accused Pelagius of reducing Christianity to a set of moral rules, and God to a moral judge; and he pronounced Pelagius a dangerous heretic for underestimating the power of sin, and thence for denying the need for a saviour. Augustine by contrast taught that the first sin of Adam is passed from one generation to the next through the sinful act of sex, so that humans are born sinners and condemned to eternal damnation. God, however, has in advance chosen a small number to be saved, through the sacrificial death of Christ on the cross.

The dispute between these two men and their respective followers grew increasingly bitter, with each side publishing vitriolic tracts against the other. Augustine proved the more skilled at getting bishops and clergy on to his side; and in 418 a council of bishops held at Carthage condemned Pelagius as a heretic. Pelagius was forced to retreat to the desert of Egypt, where he died two years later.

The ideas and vision of Pelagius are preserved in a small number of letters which he wrote to followers; none of his other writings survive. There is no evidence that any of these letters, or any of his works, found their way to Britain; nor is he referred to by name in any of the later Celtic literature. Yet the similarity between his theology and that of the Celtic church which burst into life in the sixth and seventh centuries suggests that his influence was pervasive. And to this day if the rival doctrines of Augustine and Pelagius are put to British churchgoers, the great majority opt for Pelagius.

This book contains selections from his letters, abridged and paraphrased to make them accessible to the modern reader. It is divided into eighty-four short sections, which can be read straight through, or enjoyed as daily meditations.

Robert Van de Weyer

1

Even if I were able to write with elegance and fluency, I would still feel that the present task was beyond my capacities. I must write to Demetrias, a woman who has kept herself a virgin for the sake of Christ. She is noble and rich, and yet she spurns nobility and riches. I can easily praise such a person, but I have no right to instruct her, since her moral qualities are manifestly superior to my own. She was born in the very highest station; she grew up surrounded by wealth and luxury; the pleasures of this life seemed to bind her like the strongest of chains. Yet suddenly she broke free, exchanging her material goods for spiritual goodness. With the sword of faith she cut herself off from all earthly privilege. With the nails which pinned Christ on the cross she crucified her own flesh for his sake. Not only did she choose to live without wealth, but she renounced the right to inherit wealth when her parents died; she left herself no possibility of escape.

To Demetrias

2

Demetrias is so eager to learn the way of perfection that no words of mine could meet her needs: almost as soon as I offer some new instruction, she has surpassed it. She is well aware of the wealth and honour she has spurned, the pleasures she has rejected, the privileges she has renounced; so she wants spiritual wealth and honour of even greater proportions. Compared with her desire, my life is very mediocre; compared with the divine riches to which she aspires, my teaching is cheap and shabby. She wants her love for God to be as ardent as her former love for luxury. She wants her conduct to be as noble in its moral qualities as her former life was noble in the eyes of the world. What wisdom uttered by a mere human such as myself can satisfy such hunger for truth? What power of speech can match the spiritual power she already possesses? Yet I write at her request. She is so humble that she seeks instruction from someone as poor in wisdom as I am. She asks me to water the seed which God has planted in her soul; so I have no choice but to pour as much water upon that seed as my spiritual strength permits.

To Demetrias

3

Whenever I give moral instruction , I first try to demonstrate the inherent power and quality of human nature. I try to show the wonderful virtues which all human beings can acquire. Most people look at the virtues in others, and imagine that such virtues are far beyond their reach. Yet God has implanted in every person the capacity to attain the very highest level of virtue. But people cannot grow in virtue on their own. We each need companions to guide and direct us on the way of righteousness; without such companions we are liable to stray from the firm path, and then sink into the mud of despair. At first a companion who has achieved a high level of virtue can seem utterly different from oneself. But as friendship grows, one begins to see in the companion a mirror of oneself. The reason is that, in moral capacities, God has created us all the same: we are each capable of achieving the same degree of moral goodness. Once people perceive this truth, they are filled with hope, knowing that in the fullness of time they can share the moral virtue of Christ himself.

To Demetrias

4

We measure the goodness of human nature in relation to its creator, whom we call God. When he created the world, God declared that everything he had made was good. So if every tree and animal, insect and plant is good, how much better is man himself! God made man in his own image; and so he intends each of us to be like him. God has made many animals stronger and faster than human beings. He has given many animals teeth and jaws that are more powerful and sharper than the finest sword. But he has given man intelligence and freedom. We alone are able to recognize God as our maker, and thence to understand the goodness of his creation. Thus we have the capacity to distinguish between good and evil, right and wrong. This capacity means that we do not act out of compulsion; nor need we be swayed by our immediate wants and desires, as animals are. Instead we make choices. Day by day, hour by hour, we have to reach decisions; and in each decision, we can choose good or evil. The freedom to choose makes us like God: if we choose evil, that freedom becomes a curse; if we choose good, it becomes our greatest blessing.

To Demetrias

5

Many people out of ignorance claim that man is not truly good because he is capable of doing evil. In saying this they are denying the perfect goodness of God's creation. In fact man is truly good for the very reason that these people say he is not: that he has freedom to choose good or evil. Within the heart of man there is no over-whelming compulsion to act in one way or the other; whereas animals are compelled to act according to their instinct, human beings have free will, enabling them to control their actions. And within the mind of man there is the capacity of reason: human beings are able to consider rationally the consequences of different courses of action. It is the combination of free will and rationality which makes human beings superior to all other creatures. There would be no virtue in doing good by instinct, without exercising free will and reason. But when people, after due consideration, decide to do good, then they truly share in the goodness of God.

To Demetrias

6

By granting us the wonderful gift of freedom, God gave us the capacity to do evil as well as do good. Indeed we would not be free unless God had given us this ability: there is no freedom for the person who does good by instinct and not by choice. In this sense the capacity to do evil is itself good; evil actions are themselves signs of the goodness of God. A person might say that the world would be a better place if everyone within it were always good and never evil. But such a world would be flawed because it would lack one essential attribute of goodness, namely freedom. When God created the world he was acting freely; no other force compelled God to create the world. Thus by creating human beings in his image, he had to give them freedom. A person who could only do good and never do evil would be in chains; a person who can choose good or evil shares the freedom of God.

To Demetrias

7

All of us, out of ignorance and lack of faith, sometimes wish that God had made us differently. We are like a pot saying to the potter: 'Why have you moulded me in this shape?' We wish that only good and loving emotions stirred our hearts, and that evil desires were banished. We wish that we always had the right words on our lips, and never uttered any words of malice or rudeness. We wish that we always behaved with gentleness and generosity, and were never harsh or mean. But if our emotions were always good, our words always right, our actions always kind, then we could never learn the difference between good and evil. Only by discovering within ourselves evil desires, only by speaking words of evil, only by our evil actions, do we learn the misery which evil brings. Then we have the knowledge to choose good. So let us thank God that he has given us the capacity for evil, and thence given us the freedom to choose good.

To Demetrias

8

Those who follow Christ often believe that only Christians are capable of doing good. They assert that Christianity has a monopoly of virtue. But this assertion is quite contrary to what we can observe. All of us have met pagans who are tolerant, temperate, chaste, generous and kind; and we have met pagans who reject the pleasures and honours of this world, choosing instead the way of simplicity and humility. In short we have met pagans who reflect the virtues of Christ himself. If only Christians were good, then God would not be good, because he would have denied the rest of humanity the freedom to choose goodness. The goodness we see in pagans is proof of the goodness of God. He has granted every person, regardless of race or religion, the freedom to choose good or evil. The advantage of being a Christian is that through the teaching of Jesus Christ we learn more fully the nature of goodness; and through his example, we are inspired to choose good.

To Demetrias

9

Come now to the secret places of the soul. Let us each inspect ourselves with care, looking at the emotions which stir our hearts and the thoughts which run through our minds. Let us learn the essential goodness of the heart from the heart itself; let us learn the goodness of the mind from the mind itself. Why do we blush with guilt or tremble with fear whenever we commit a sin? Because our hearts and minds are good, and so recoil from evil. Why do we shine with joy and dance with delight whenever we do good? Because our hearts and minds are good, and so rejoice at every good action. A murderer may try to conceal his identity, but the torments of his conscience are worse than any punishment which the state authorities could inflict. An innocent man who is wrongly accused of some crime may be imprisoned and tortured; but even when his body cries out with pain, there will be peace and serenity within his soul, because his conscience is clear.

To Demetrias

10

Within our minds there is a kind of natural sanctity, which we call conscience. This conscience presides over the mind as a judge presides over a court. It favours honourable and righteous actions, and it condemns hurtful and wrong actions. Just as a judge is guided by a book of law, so the conscience is guided by an inner law which has been written on the soul by God. But in one important respect the way in which conscience works is different from the way a court works. In a court lawyers on opposing sides try to win their case by brilliant argument; they are not trying to reveal the truth, but merely to win the judge to their side. Conscience, by contrast, rejects brilliant argument, and instead wants only the truth of each and every situation; and only when it has discerned the truth will conscience make its judgement. When we read scriptures and remark that Moses or Abraham were good people, we are simply saying that in them conscience was a firm and strong judge.

To Demetrias

11

When Adam and Eve ate from the tree of knowledge they were exercising their freedom of choice; and as a consequence of the choice they made, they were no longer able to live in the Garden of Eden. When we hear that story we are struck by their disobedience to God; and so we conclude that they were no longer fit to enjoy the perfect happiness of Eden. And we should also be struck by the nature of that tree and its fruit. Before eating the fruit they did not know the difference between good and evil; thus they did not possess the knowledge which enables human beings to exercise freedom of choice. By eating the fruit they acquired this knowledge, and from that moment onwards they were free. Thus the story of their banishment from Eden is in truth the story of how the human race gained its freedom: by eating fruit from the tree of knowledge, Adam and Eve became mature human beings, responsible to God for their actions.

To Demetrias

12

How is it possible, then, for an act of disobedience to God to bring such a blessing? When Adam and Eve lived in the Garden of Eden they were like small children: they simply obeyed God's instructions without considering the moral reasons for those instructions. To become mature they needed to learn the distinction for themselves between right and wrong, good and evil. And God gave them the opportunity to become mature by putting within the garden the tree of knowledge, by which they could learn this distinction. But if God had simply instructed Adam and Eve to eat from the tree, and they had obeyed, they would have been acting like children. So he forbade them from eating the fruit; this meant that they themselves had to make a decision, whether to eat or not to eat. Just as a young person needs to defy his parents in order to grow to maturity, so Adam and Eve needed to defy God in order to share his knowledge of good and evil. By defying God, Adam and Eve grew to maturity in his image.

To Demetrias

13

We sometimes point to particular people, and say that those people are incapable of doing good; they seem so corrupt that they are compelled to be malicious and evil. We point to other people, and say that they are incapable of doing evil; they seem so kind, gentle and generous in spirit that they are compelled to do good. In truth no one is totally evil nor totally good; every person at every moment is capable of choosing good or choosing evil. Yet habit is very important. If a person gets into the habit of choosing evil, then at each moment of choice his inclination will be to choose evil again. Equally if a person gets into the habit of choosing good, then at each moment of choice his inclination will be to choose good again. So as parents we should encourage our children to get into good habits. And we ourselves should retain good habits. If we habitually choose good, then it is much easier to make right choices in the future.

To Demetrias

14

When we read the stories of the Old Testament, we see what a bumpy path the Hebrew people had to travel. Although they had numerous written laws, they were often confused about the inner spiritual law of good and evil. Thus they frequently committed acts of terrible cruelty and injustice. Yet they were not ignorant or stupid. God puts the inner spritual law on every person's heart; and many of the great leaders and prophets were extremely proficient at discerning the spiritual law. For this reason we can admire their wonderful holiness. We by contrast have a much smoother road to travel. In the person of Jesus Christ the inner spiritual law is made fully manifest for us. His words explain the spiritual law, and his life and death exemplify it. Through him we are reborn as new men and women, because we can see clearly how we should live. We no longer need outer written laws, because in Christ we understand fully the inner spiritual law.

To Demetrias

15

When a wife wants to please her husband, she finds out what her husband wants, and acts accordingly. A husband wanting to please his wife acts in the same way. As human beings our first desire should be to please God. He created us in his own image; and for this reason true joy consists in loving him, as a husband loves his wife and a wife loves her husband. And in order to love and please God, we must find out what he wants; we must discern his will. In the teachings and the example of Jesus Christ we learn the general principles of behaviour which pleases God. Then, at each moment of choice, we must apply those principles in practice. To do this God has given us two vital tools. The first is reason: we can use reason to work out how God's spiritual law applies in each and every situation. The second is prayer: we can talk to God, asking him to guide our thoughts. We can be sure that, if we consider every choice carefully, and if we seek divine guidance, our decisions will please God.

To Demetrias

16

A person may pray at length before each decision, and may think deeply, weighing up all the possible consequences; and yet later it seems that he made the wrong decision. God possesses perfect reason, so he can see all the consequences of every possible decision. Since human reason is partial and imperfect, we invariably fail to anticipate all the consequences of our decisions; so without any evil or malicious intentions, a decision may hurt or damage others. Does this mean that God has not answered our prayers? Does it mean that he has not guided our thoughts? The world is exceedingly complex; so the decisions made by one person cannot be judged in isolation, but must be seen in the context of the hundreds and thousands of decisions being made by others at the same time. Even if one person reaches a decision with good intentions, those intentions may be undermined by the bad intentions of others. It is for this reason that good decisions may seem sometimes to have bad consequences. What matters is that each person thinks, decides and acts with a pure conscience.

To Demetrias

17

A person may make a decision without prayer or serious thought; and yet that decision seems to have good consequences. A person may even make a decision with evil intentions, and good consequences may flow from it. Does this mean that the world which God has created is irrational? Does it mean that God himself cannot distinguish between good and evil? Again we must remember how complex the world is. Human society is like a spider's web; and if you pull only one tiny thread of the web, the shape of the entire web changes. Our small minds cannot begin to grasp this complexity. Yet we can observe how evil intentions do indeed sometimes have good consequences: a person may intend to hurt and damage other people, and yet does them a service. This is surely the greatest miracle of God's creation. He has so designed and ordered things that there is a natural tendency towards good and away from evil. Thus even our evil intentions can be thwarted by the benign genius of God.

To Demetrias

18

It is important to distinguish that which is good from that which is perfect. For example a good person may eat meat and drink wine; but perfection requires a person to abstain from meat and wine. A good person may enjoy a degree of wealth and luxury; but perfection requires a person to live with as few material possessions as is compatible with survival. A good person may marry, enjoying the comfort and the pleasure which marriage brings; but perfection requires a person to be celibate. God has created all things for our enjoyment; and therefore physical pleasure is good. Yet the person who seeks perfection acquires more and more pleasure from less and less. The perfect person derives the greatest pleasure from the simplest food. The perfect person rejoices in a tiny hut with a few sticks of furniture. The perfect person sees beauty in every human being, so has no need to possess the beauty of a spouse. Contrary to what some religious leaders teach, perfection is not the denial of pleasure, but the enhancement of it.

To Demetrias

19

Do not be deceived by those who seem to seek perfection, yet do not keep the basic commandments of God. There are people who eat little, who live simply and who are celibate; yet they show no love and compassion towards their neighbours. Before seeking perfection a person must first learn to love others and to be generous towards them. This world would be a most wonderful place if everyone was loving and generous, yet no one sought perfection; perfection is, as it were, a spiritual luxury, not a necessity. So even if you do aspire towards perfection, do not neglect the basic duties of love. If you see someone who is hungry, share your food. If you see someone who is thirsty, share your drink. If you see someone weeping, offer comfort. If you see someone in despair, offer hope. If you see someone utterly confused and bewildered, try to understand the confusion and then seek clarity. Unless you are loving and generous in these ways, seeking perfection is like trying to build a magnificent palace without first putting in strong foundations.

To Demetrias

20

If you were besotted with the things of this world, you would want to surpass all others in the luxury of your house, in the magnificence of your garments and jewelry, in the abundance of food on your table, in the splendour of the carriage which took you from one place to another. You would never be satisfied with what you already possessed, but would always want more. And you would constantly be comparing yourself with others, looking with envy at those even richer than you. Your wealth would be like a spiritual prison; and your limitless desires would be the chains that bound you. Thus in giving up all these things, you have smashed the chains and broken free. You have little; yet you are satisfied with what you have. You are poorer than most; yet you feel no envy towards the riches of others. To you a simple tunic is like a royal robe; a tiny hut is like a palace; a bowl of porridge is like a feast; a pair of sandals is like a golden carriage.

To Demetrias

21

As one looks around at friends and neighbours, one sees great enthusiasm and ambition. There are people who love to write, and each is ambitious to become the finest writer in the world. There are people who love political power, and each wants to attain the very highest ambition. There are people who relish military glory, and each wants to lead an army to a famous victory. There are people who enjoy buying and selling, and each wants to become the richest person in their city. There are people who keep animals, and each wants the finest herd of cattle or sheep in their region. We must admit that civilisation depends on men of ambition, whose enthusiasm and energy create prosperity and security for everyone. Yet how very few people are enthusiastic about holiness, and are ambitious to become saints. If the world is to become truly civilized we need far more people with holiness as their aim. They radiate joy and love which all can share.

To Demetrias

22

People love feasts. They love to prepare huge amounts of rich food, and to choose the finest wine; the excitement of preparing a feast is an important part of its pleasure. Then on the appointed day they love to gather in a great crowd, to sing and dance, and then to eat the food and drink the wine. When a child is born people hold feasts; when a young man and woman get married their families hold a feast; when a person dies, his or her children have a feast. There are feasts to celebrate military victories. And there are feasts to mark all the great religious anniversaries. It is good and natural that people should enjoy feasts, because they are a sign of the greatest feast of all, to which God invites us: the feast in his heavenly kingdom around his throne. There the singing and dancing, the eating and drinking, will last for all eternity. But we do not need to prepare food and choose wine for this heavenly feast; we need to prepare ourselves by learning always to choose righteousness.

To Demetrias

23

During the first five years of a child's life the parents should devote every effort to instilling good and holy habits. Just as a sapling is supple and flexible, and so can be directed in one way or another by means of tying it to a strong stick, so the soul of a child is supple and flexible, and can be directed towards good or evil by strong discipline. But if a person has been brought up by weak or bad parents, and so has not acquired good habits, all is not lost. Even a mature tree can be induced to grow in a new direction by means of careful pruning. All actions which arise from bad habits or intentions must cease. At first the soul will cry with pain, just as a tree, if it had feelings, would cry with pain when branches are pruned. But if bad actions cease, then eventually the heart and the soul will change. The person will no longer have evil thoughts and emotions, and instead will begin to feel love and compassion towards others.

To Demetrias

24

Your family has produced many great men. It has provided generals whose military prowess thrilled the entire world. It has provided consuls whose wisdom and firmness in the exercise of power has been widely admired and imitated. It has provided lawyers whose passion for truth and justice has struck fear in the hearts of criminals and gratitude in the hearts of the innocent. When you were born, your mother and grandmother looked forward to your marrying a general, a consul or a lawyer of similar repute. So when you told them of your intention to remain a virgin, and to devote yourself to prayer and good works, they were at first bitterly disappointed. But it is to their great credit that they now support you in your way of life. They can see that the seeds of goodness which they sowed within you as a child are now bearing a rich harvest. Your mother would have liked a harvest of grandchildren; but she is now taking even greater pleasure in a harvest of virtue.

To Demetrias

25

Inevitably when we read the scriptures, some of the sayings of Christ strike us as especially important, while we ignore other sayings. Our minds select those sayings which suit our particular needs and desires. To some degree this process of selection is right. At each period in our lives we need to concentrate on some particular aspects of Christ's teaching; we cannot acquire all the virtues at once, so we focus our attention on one or two virtues at a time. But we must beware of selecting only those passages of scripture which we find congenial, while remaining blind to those which are difficult. As we walk in the footsteps of Christ, the road becomes increasingly rough and bumpy. At the beginning we acquire virtues which come easily to us; but later we must acquire virtues which are much harder. We will be tempted to stop and even turn back; but that would mean turning our faces away from Christ. Once we have started along his road, we must continue until we reach the end – which is heaven.

To Demetrias

26

When you decided to follow the path of holiness, you accepted – indeed you embraced – Jesus Christ as your guide. You did not know where the path would lead; you had no maps, nor had you ever travelled on that path before. So you had to rely on Jesus completely, obeying his commands without question. Every person who decides to travel on this path must make the same act of obedience. Yet obedience brings a new temptation: to grumble. A person who has control over his life may be selfish and greedy, but does not grumble, because he cannot blame anyone else for his own discomforts and misfortunes. But a person who has submitted himself to the will of another – as you have submitted to Christ – is tempted to complain and to grumble at even the most minor discomfort. Do not be surprised if you feel tempted to grumble at Jesus, complaining of the humps and the bumps on the road to holiness. But resist that temptation: he would not cause you any discomfort unless it was necessary for the good of your soul.

To Demetrias

27

The person who makes evil choices is stupid and foolish. The person who makes good choices is intelligent and wise. Evil people often pride themselves on their cunning plans and their crafty schemes; they congratulate themselves on being able to outwit others. Yet even when their plans and schemes succeed, they derive no real pleasure and joy. So in fact they are stupid, acting against their own true interests. Good people by contrast are straight and honest, and they recoil from any plan which is crooked and devious, preferring only to do things which may benefit their neighbours. Yet even when their efforts seem to fail, they can still enjoy a peaceful conscience; and when their efforts succeed, they rejoice in the happiness which others derive. So good people are intelligent, acting in their own true interests. And when we confront a bad person, there is little point in showing outrage or even disapproval. Instead we should try to open their eyes, so that they can see that the most effective way to be selfish is to be unselfish; that in doing good to others you earn the greatest rewards.

To Demetrias

28

The most cunning strategy which the devil uses against those who aspire to holiness is depression. Those who devote themselves to outward, worldly ambitions are lifted from depression by the stimulus of physical pleasure. Those who devote themselves to spiritual ambitions reject this stimulus, in order to find a deeper source of joy. But there is a long gap between rejecting the pleasures of the world and receiving the fullness of joy which comes from God. During this long gap people can easily begin to despair; and their souls can sink into lethargy and melancholy. Depression of the spirit can become like a thick black cloud which even the light of Christ cannot penetrate. Sometimes the cloud lifts of its own accord. But more often the person must make an initial effort to blow it away. There is only one means of doing this: prayer. Through constantly talking to God, and trying to hear him, we eventually receive a taste of his heavenly joy; and even the smallest taste can restore our spiritual energy and ambition. So when you feel depressed, pray even harder and more constantly than when you feel happy.

To Demetrias

29

A second strategy which the devil uses to induce people to do evil is speed. A feeling can enter a person's heart, a thought can enter the mind, and this feeling and thought can lead to an action being done all within a matter of seconds. So although a person always has the freedom and the power to choose between good and evil, speed can prevent that freedom and power being properly exercised. Indeed most evil actions are done impetuously, without serious thought. Thus if you are to be sure always to do good, you must learn to be slow, giving yourself time to reflect on your emotions, and to consider carefully the consequences of different courses of action. Only act when you know that your emotions are pure, and that you have assessed as fully as possible the consequences of your action. In this way you will be certain of defeating the devil.

To Demetrias

Two kinds of thought go through our minds. The first are thoughts which are clear and deliberate, which involve the faculty of reason. Such thoughts may stay within the mind for many minutes, hours and days; indeed this kind of thought may constantly recur over a whole lifetime. The second are thoughts which are mere impressions, flitting through the mind like insubstantial shadows. These thoughts may only remain within the mind for a few seconds. A person who wishes to do good has nothing to fear from the first kind of thought. There is ample time to hone and to shape such thoughts, to ensure that they conform to God's law. The second kind of thought, however, is potentially more dangerous. In the case of a person in the habit of doing good, impressions will tend to be benign; but even within a good person the devil can easily distort impressions to give them a malicious twist. In the case of a person with evil habits, impressions will generally be malign. A person who acts on impressions becomes the slave of them, failing to exercise freedom of choice. A person who truly wants to be free must never act on impressions; then he will become their master.

To Demetrias

31

A third strategy which the devil uses is complacency. As we grow in goodness, we are tempted to congratulate ourselves on our progress. We compare our present level of moral achievement with our past level, and we feel satisfied with the success of our efforts. Worse still we compare ourselves with other people, thinking that we are morally far superior to most of those whom we know. It may indeed be true that we have made giant strides on the way of Christ; it may also be true that we are far ahead of most other people. Yet we must not allow such thoughts to fill our minds. The further a person travels along the way of holiness, the further he realizes the road ahead stretches. When a person first sets out on the road, he imagines that after a short distance he will be almost perfect. But with each pace a person takes, he sees two more paces ahead. Thus as we make progress, we should become less, not more, complacent. We should become more, not less, aware of our faults and failures.

To Demetrias

32

A fourth strategy which the devil uses is myopia: making the immediate future seem more important than the distant future. The nature of human desire is that immediate joys and pleasures seem very attractive; and we feel impelled to follow our desires. Often this is quite right: if a person is hungry, he should eat; if a person is cold, he should go and sit near a fire. But sometimes it is wrong. A person may be on fire with sexual desire; yet to satisfy that desire could mean committing adultery or breaking a vow of perpetual virginity. A person may be on fire with desire for gold; yet to satisfy that desire could involve dishonesty and fraud. In both cases the long-term consequence would be terrible, leading eventually to punishment at the hands of God himself. The devil, however, puts into the mind all sorts of reasons for submitting to evil desire; the devil may even convince the mind that God himself sanctions illicit sexual behaviour or greed for gold. In this way all thought for the longer-term consequences is pushed from the mind. The way to defeat this strategy is, at every moment of choice, to look at both the immediate and the distant consequences of each course of action, and to give distant consequences as much weight as immediate ones.

To Demetrias

33

Of all the emotions and desires within the human breast, the one that is most often misunderstood and misused is ambition. This emotion distinguishes us from all the other creatures which inhabit the world. An animal, bird, fish or insect has no ambition; it simply looks for food in order to sustain itself for another day. But the human being can look ahead, anticipating the consequences far into the future of present actions. And our ambitions determine the course of our present actions. Ambition in itself is neither good nor bad; what matters is how it is directed. Ambition may be directed towards the accumulation of power and wealth, towards material superiority over others. Such ambition is evil, because power and wealth can only be gained at the expense of others. Or ambition may be directed towards holiness and moral perfection, towards becoming like Christ himself. The emotion which lusts after power and wealth is the same as the emotion which yearns for holiness and perfection; the difference lies in the way in which the emotion is directed.

To Demetrias

34

To a small child every week seems like a year. To a young man or woman every year seems like a decade. To an old person every decade seems like a year. As we grow older, the days, weeks, months and years seem to pass more quickly. This is a sign that as we grow older, we also grow wiser. Our life on earth is very short compared with eternity: it is no more than the blink of an eye. We should constantly remind ourselves of the shortness of earthly life, and thence the proximity of death. The pleasures and joys of this world are trivial and fleeting, and so are the pains and the sorrows. But the joy of heaven, which is the reward for making good and wise choices on earth, lasts for all eternity. And the agony of hell, which is the punishment for making bad choices on earth, also lasts for all eternity. The day of judgement, when God will decide where to send us, is imminent; even if a person is young, and destined to live for a hundred years, the day is still imminent. By remembering this truth day by day, you will always make good choices.

To Demetrias

35

I am writing to you at great length, and I hope that much of what I say is of value to you. Yet I know that most of the words which are spoken or written in this world are useless or even harmful; and I must admit that the same may be true of my words. We should each be discreet and sparing in our words. We should only speak and write when we are sure that our motives are pure, and that our words will do good to those who hear or read them. Let our speech always be modest and calm; let sweetness mix with dignity; let wisdom mingle with modesty. Let us be firm in what we say, and yet also fair, seeing both sides of every argument. Let us use words and phrases which most aptly convey our meaning to those who are listening to us. Let us never be pompous or self-important in our speech, and never resort to harsh words. If I have been guilty of pomposity or harshness in what I have written to you, please forgive me.

To Demetrias

36

You are a spiritual infant. You have just decided to make
Jesus Christ your master, obeying him in all things. Yet
you know so little of what he taught, and you understand
even less. Thus although you want to obey him and to
abide by his laws, you do not know how. Since you are
an infant, I will feed you milk. I will not risk confusing
you with complex theological and moral arguments, but
I will only use the simplest concepts and ideas. Yet this
does not mean that you will receive an inferior version of
the gospel. In truth every disciple of Christ, even those
who have been disciples for many decades, are infants.
On this earth we only have glimmers of the truth; only
narrow shafts of divine light pierce the veil that separates
heaven from earth. So the teaching of Jesus Christ is
simple; and those who try to use the complex logic of
philosophy to interpret his teaching are distorting it. So
the milk which I will feed you is the same milk which
nourishes me; it is the milk which Jesus himself gives.

To a new Christian

Jesus tells us that when a person decides to become his disciple, that person is born anew. Yet when we look at a new disciple, he looks exactly the same as he did before his decision. Also within his heart the old emotions and desires still flow; and through his mind old thoughts continue to pass. Yet that single decision to become a Christian alters the direction in which a person is facing. He commits himself to filling his mind with the words of Jesus, so that his thoughts will constantly be influenced by those words. When a baby is born, his entire life is directed towards becoming an adult; yet the process of growing from infancy to adulthood takes two decades. When a person is born anew in the gospel, his entire life is directed towards becoming like Jesus; yet the process of growing from being an ordinary sinner to the moral and spiritual perfection of Jesus takes all the years remaining to that person on earth – and more beyond death.

To a new Christian

As a disciple of Christ you cannot be half-hearted. It is impossible to be half saved and half condemned. You cannot choose to obey half of Christ's teaching and reject the other half. Your intentions cannot be half good and half bad. You must decide to follow Christ with your whole heart. You must commit yourself to study his teaching and to obey it. At each moment of decision, you must sincerely seek to discern the will of God. If you are half-hearted you will not in fact achieve anything: the devil will take a firm grip of one half of the heart, and use it to subjugate the other half. Moreover you cannot understand one part of Christ's teaching without understanding the whole of his teaching: the different parts are tied together like the threads of a spider's web. If you constantly try to compromise, finding some middle path between the way of Christ and the way of the world, you will become confused and lost. Jesus never compromised; neither should you.

To a new Christian

39

God forgives all sins. His grace can discharge you from all the wrongs you have committed. You deserve to be punished for many of the things you have done. Yet in his mercy God will set aside all punishment. This is the good news which Christ preached, and which his apostles carried across the world. It was to reveal this divine truth that Christ died on the cross. But you must give your consent to God's mercy. God can only forgive you if you repent of your sins. This means that you must describe to God the wrongs you have committed, and promise that you will make every effort to avoid repeating those wrongs in the future. You will not always fulfil your good intentions: through force of habit you may commit old sins. Then you must confess these sins again to God, and promise again to try and avoid them in the future. Little by little your old sinful habits will die, and new virtuous habits will take their place. So little by little your repentance will become more complete.

To a new Christian

40

Every day men and women die. Any day your life may end. You may suddenly be taken ill, and within a few hours the breath may leave your body. An accident may befall you, and in a single second your life on earth is snuffed out. You have become a Christian partly because you believe that the teaching of Christ is right here on earth; that the only way to attain true joy on earth is to follow Christ. And you have become a Christian partly because you wish to please God, so that when you die he will receive you into his heavenly kingdom. This second reason reinforces the first. When you are tempted to stray from the path of Christ you need only remind yourself how close death is; you need only tell yourself that within a few hours or even seconds you could be standing at the throne of divine judgement, answering for your actions. So I strongly urge you to remind yourself day by day of the fragility of earthly life, and thence put your trust in the eternal permanence of life in heaven.

To a new Christian

41

Christians often speak of the sacrifices a person must make in following Christ. They point to the sacrifice of Christ on the cross, and they say that in smaller ways every Christian should imitate his sacrifice. It is true that in following Christ a person must sacrifice all desire for wealth, status and power, and commit himself to serving the needs of others. It is also true that Christians are sometimes required to suffer physical injuries, even death itself, for their faith. Yet to emphasize sacrifice is to upset the balance of the faith. Christ's death on the cross would have been a pointless and meaningless sacrifice, had he not risen from death on the third day. This pattern applies to every sacrifice. Even the smallest act of self-denial, in the service of others, brings joy which far exceeds any pain or discomfort which has been endured. You have become a disciple of Christ not because you want to suffer pain, but because you want to share his joy. And you will only have the courage and resilience to make sacrifices if your eyes remain firmly fixed on the joy which Jesus promises.

To a new Christian

42

As a new Christian you inevitably pride yourself on your achievements. You have already learnt many of the commandments of Jesus, and with great zeal you have been putting them into practice. Your family, your friends and your neighbours are probably amazed at the change that has come over you; and their reaction increases your pride. You are also praying to God with great fervour, and you feel very close to him; and you are astonished at how readily and how quickly he answers your prayers. This pride which you feel is right and good. A Christian should always feel proud of his faith, and so be willing to boast to others about the power and the glory of Jesus Christ. But beware that pride in your faith does not become pride in your own achievements. The line between boasting about the power of Christ, and boasting about your own spiritual power, is easily crossed. When you find yourself reflecting on the changes that have taken place in your life since becoming a disciple of Christ, ensure that these reflections always lead to gratitude to God. A heart that is truly grateful can never be a proud heart.

To a new Christian

43

God is always especially kind and generous to new disciples of Christ. He answers their prayers almost as soon as those prayers have been uttered. He gives special strength to enable new Christians to obey the commandments of Christ with ease. He fills the hearts of new disciples with joyful fervour. When a man and a woman get married, the early months of their life together are usually intensely happy, and every problem is easily surmounted. In the same way the early months of faith are intensely happy, and all things seem possible. But in a marriage this first ardour cools, and the couple must acquire a quieter and more enduring love. Similarly the ardour of new faith soon cools. God is no longer so speedy in answering prayers. Fresh obstacles appear which hinder the new Christian in his obedience to Christ. At this point some disciples fall away, turning their backs on Christ; they regard their early faith as a foolish illusion. Others, however, acquire a quieter and more enduring love for Christ.

To a new Christian

44

You are now at this point of change. Since becoming a disciple of Christ you have been with him on a high mountain; now he is leading you down the slopes to the plain below. On the mountain the air was fresh and pure, the ground firm and hard, the sky bright and clear. Now on the plains the air is damp and heavy, the lanes are muddy and rough, the sky grey and cloudy. If you remain loyal to Christ he will from time to time take you up the mountain again, in order to refresh your faith. But most of your life will be on the plain. When you were high on the mountain you began to look with pity, even a little contempt, at the Christians on the plain. You said to yourself that their prayers were less fervent than yours, their hearts less ardent than yours. Now you are learning that true faith does not consist in fervour, and true love does not consist in ardour.

To a new Christian

45

God is present in all things, great and small. God's power is manifest in all events, great and small. So you do not need to involve yourself in great matters in order to serve God. You can serve him in small matters, in the mundane concerns of daily life. So if you plough the soil in a spirit of love, you are serving God. If you care for your cattle and sheep in a spirit of love, you are serving God. If you treat your servants with generosity, you are serving God. If you build a house for your family, you are serving God. If you speak at a public forum with words of wisdom, you are serving God. If you cherish your wife and your children, you are serving God. Perhaps in the fullness of time God will call you to some great act: he may require you to be leader of a Christian congregation; he may ask you to suffer and even to die for your faith. And if such a call comes, you must be ready to hear it and respond. But in the meantime obey God in the ordinary things of life.

To a new Christian

46

Often Christians try to distinguish between major offences against God's law and minor ones. They say that such things as murder, stealing and adultery are major offences; whereas speaking rudely or harshly, and being mean with money are minor offences. While there is some truth in this distinction, it easily becomes an excuse for moral indiscipline. People feel satisfied with themselves for avoiding the major offences, and feel little or no guilt at the minor offences they commit. Moreover an offence which may appear minor can do terrible harm. Harsh and rude words can wound another person's soul as severely as a dagger can wound the body. A person who is rich, and yet refuses to give food to the hungry, may cause far more deaths than even the cruellest murderer. So it is better to make no distinction between major and minor offences. Instead we should try to obey God's law in all matters, great and small.

To a new Christian

47

You ask me whether it would be better for you to become a monk, living alone in some remote place and devoting yourself wholly to prayer. You are a married man, so you could only consider such a course with your wife's consent. Yet even to ask her consent is to suggest that you are not happy with her company, and so could cause her great offence. Moreover consent is not sufficient; she must actually want you to live as a monk. And she will only want this if she herself wants also to live alone. Yet all these questions are premature. As a new Christian, you want every aspect of your life to be transformed in the light of your faith. Yet Jesus is concerned primarily with your soul; the transformation which he wants is inside you. It is possible that he wants the exterior aspects of your life to remain unchanged. Indeed a person can devote himself wholly to Christ in any and every circumstance.

To a new Christian

48

From the moment you decided to be a disciple of Christ until now you have been certain of your faith. You have accepted without question everything that you have found in the New Testament, and all the doctrines of the church. You feel sure that you have grasped the truth. But soon doubts will creep into your mind. You will start questioning things you read in scripture; you will start arguing about particular doctrines. One doubt will lead to another, until faith itself will seem no more than a rickety old house which could be blown over at any time. Yet these doubts are the foundation stones for a firm and robust faith. You will realize that doctrines are inventions of the human mind, as it tries to penetrate the mystery of God. You will realize that scripture itself is the work of human minds, recording the example and the teaching of Jesus. Thus it is not what you believe that matters; it is how you respond with your heart and your actions. It is not believing in Christ that matters; it is becoming like him.

To a new Christian

49

When he walked from village to village speaking to the
ordinary people he met, Jesus did not ask people to
accept high-flown doctrines. In fact he did not ask them
to believe anything. Instead he asked them to enter a
relationship with God. He told them that if they prayed
to God as a loving father, God would fill them with
wisdom and strength. And he said that if they acted
according to God's love, they would experience joy and
peace in this life and the next. The proof of his teaching
was his own example: through constant prayer he was
supremely strong and wise; and by choosing to obey God
in all things, he overflowed with joy. The proof too lay
in the example of all those who followed his teaching.
Do not let your mind be seduced by theological specula-
tion; the human mind can never grasp the supreme glory
of God. Simply follow Jesus wherever he leads.

To a new Christian

50

I am not worthy to offer you guidance. I have no special insights, nor can I claim to be holy. You have asked me for advice, and I will reply, not because I regard myself as superior to you, but because I regard you as superior. Therefore if you ask something of me, I must assume your request is wise. A man who refuses to drink from the stream running past him, but instead looks for a purer stream elsewhere, may be thirsty, but is not very thirsty. A man who refuses a loaf of brown bread, but instead waits until white bread is available, may be hungry, but not very hungry. You, however, must be very thirsty and hungry in spirit to ask my advice on spiritual matters, because if you searched more widely you could find far better spiritual counsellors. Yet perhaps it is my weakness and my folly which attracts you. A weak and foolish man appreciates highly every small shred of wisdom he acquires, and so is eager to share those shreds with others. So I will eagerly share my few shreds with you.

To a mature Christian

51

The word 'Christ' means 'anointed one'. Until the time of Jesus Christ only very few people were deemed worthy of anointment; and through being anointed each one became prophet, priest or king. The anointment of Jesus Christ was special. Those before him had been anointed by men; Jesus was anointed by God. Those before him were anointed to one of these three offices; Jesus was anointed to all three. Jesus was a prophet through whom God spoke to the people. He was a priest through whom God's grace was channelled to the people. And he was a king, who pronounced God's law to the people. He was special in one further way also. By his anointment all who believe in him are anointed. He makes us members of his body, the church. And the church is called to be prophetic, proclaiming God's message; priestly, channelling God's grace to the world; and royal, exemplifying God's law. Individually none of us is worthy of anointment. But together we become like Jesus, anointed by God himself.

To a mature Christian

52

There are some people who do not in their hearts want to be Christian, but simply want to be called Christian. They do not want to abide by Christ's law of love. They are too proud to confess and repent of their sins, or to forgive the sins of others. They refuse to spend time in prayer, always making excuses. In short they do not want to be changed. Yet they wear the title 'Christian' with pride. They want to be treated by others with respect, as upright, honest and respectable citizens. They want people to believe that they are good and kind. And while they do not pray, they appear regularly at public worship, so that others can think them devout. Such Christianity is not merely useless, it is positively harmful. These people are mocking and insulting Jesus himself. And in this way they are making a mockery of Jesus in the eyes of others. Seeing such hypocrites, people start to regard Christianity itself as hypocritical. It is far better that people should hate and revile the Christian faith, persecuting those who profess it, than they should dismiss it as a sham.

To a mature Christian

53

God is infinitely patient. He leaves sinners undisturbed in their sin. He leaves hypocrites undisturbed in their hypocrisy. He has to be patient because he has given humankind freedom. So if people choose to remain sinful, he cannot override their choice; if people choose to be hypocrites, he cannot force them to be honest. Yet in granting humankind freedom, he also provides humankind with sufficient knowledge to make rational choices. That is why he sent Jesus Christ. In Jesus people can see clearly what a good and holy life is like: so they can make a rational choice whether to accept or reject goodness and holiness. Jesus in turn has commissioned his disciples to tell others about him. So our task is to ensure that the entire world understands, through the example of Jesus, the nature of goodness and holiness. We have no power to persuade or force people to become disciples. We can only inform them about Jesus, and then let them choose freely whether to follow his example or not.

To a mature Christian

54

God wants every person to repent of their sins, and to follow the path of goodness and holiness. He has not decided, as some contend, to save some and condemn others; he wants to save everyone. And he is prepared to wait as long as necessary for a person to repent. Indeed we are assured that death itself does not break God's patience. A person may die a sinner, yet even after death God continues to wait for that person to repent. Does this mean that no one will ultimately be condemned? Will everyone eventually turn from their sins and be saved? The answers to these questions are beyond our earthly knowledge. Yet even if it were true that everyone will eventually be saved, this would be no reason to delay repentance. Sin brings its own punishment: sinners may enjoy many material pleasures, but their hearts are empty and dark. Equally goodness brings its own reward: good people may live with few material goods, but their hearts are bright and filled with joy.

To a mature Christian

55

We know that God forgives all sins, that even the worst sinner can be saved. Yet we should not conclude from this that past sins do not matter. Two factors induce a person to sin: choice and habit. At every moment a person is free to choose good or evil. But the more often a person chooses evil, the more habitual evil becomes – and thence the more difficult it is to choose good. The habitual sinner is like the man who drinks excessive quantities of wine. At any moment he may choose to drink less, and thus become sober. But the more he drinks, the more he wants, and so the more difficult it becomes to restrain himself. In the same way the more a person sins, the more he wants to sin, and the more difficult it becomes to restrain himself. Equally the more often a person chooses to do what is right, the more he loves and appreciates what is good and holy, and so the easier it becomes to make right choices in the future.

To a mature Christian

56

There is no follower of Christ who is not at times perplexed by the suffering of good men and women. When we see a bad person suffer, we can interpret it as punishment for sin. So if an evil man contracts a painful and fatal illness when he is still young, if his house burns to the ground, if he loses his wealth in some dishonest transaction, we feel that justice is being done. But if a good man falls fatally ill in his youth, if an honest and hard-working man becomes destitute, we are indignant. We cannot understand how God can permit such injustice. Yet our indignation arises from the superficiality of our knowledge. We see pain and pleasure, sorrow and joy, in shallow, material terms. Yet a good person, who is enduring great physical distress, still senses the serene peace of God deep within his soul. The loyal disciple of Christ who is compelled to live in poverty knows that he is sharing the poverty of Christ. And the scriptures assure us that in poverty and in agony the soul of Christ knew the heavenly joy of God.

To a mature Christian

57

You and I have both been disciples of Christ for many years. We are familiar with the teaching of Christ; indeed, we know his words by heart. We have been accustomed to making decisions in the light of that teaching. Each evening, when we review the events of the day, we test and judge our actions by the standards which Jesus set. In general we can both claim to have the habit of doing good. Yet there are particular aspects of life where we both remain stubborn. And this is true of even the best and holiest of people. Perhaps a person eats or drinks to excess, and refuses to restrain his appetite. Perhaps a person has a quick and harsh temper, and refuses to control his anger. Perhaps a person needs to be the leader in every situation, and cannot take advice or criticism, nor defer to the superior judgement of others. Compared with the many other areas in which a person is good and holy, these stubborn areas may seem quite trivial. Yet if they remain unchecked, they can corrode a person's soul and blot his record.

To a mature Christian

58

How can we conquer the stubbornness in our hearts? How can we soften those hard areas? When a woman kneads dough to make bread, she finds with her fingers the lumps of flour and breaks them down. In the same way we must seek out the stubborn lumps in our souls, and break them down. This means we must be honest with ourselves, recognising clearly those areas of our lives which have not yielded to Christ. And we must each encourage our friends to be honest with us, asking them to help us see ourselves as we really are. Indeed we each need one special friend, who may be called a friend of the soul. We must open our souls completely to this friend, hiding nothing and revealing everything. And we must allow this friend to assess and judge what he sees. At times we may feel angry and even hateful towards this friend of the soul; but to turn our backs on him would be to reject God himself.

To a mature Christian

59

No one needs to be told the difference between right and wrong, good and evil; it is already written on that part of the soul which we call conscience. Yet everyone needs to be inspired to choose good and reject evil; everyone needs examples of goodness which reveal the peace and joy that come from a righteous life. The proof of both these propositions is shown whenever a person acts in a truly good and selfless fashion. When a person is willing to die for his faith, with words of forgiveness towards his executioners on his lips, everyone who watches is impressed and inspired. When a person gives generously to the poor and needy, and takes widows and orphans into his home, everyone knows that his actions are good and holy. People do not argue about whether generosity and forgiveness are good or bad; they know that they are good. People do not argue about whether they should act in the same way; deep in their hearts they want to be generous and forgiving. So every good act can inspire acts of goodness in others.

To a mature Christian

Even as Christians we are frequently tempted to use guile; and we are adept at justifying ourselves when we do. A person may tell a lie, saying to himself that his reason is to avoid hurting someone. A person who wants to get his way in an argument may keep some fact which goes against him hidden. A person may use shady or even dishonest means of gaining money, saying to himself that his needs and those of his family are greater than those of his victims. Yet none of these justifications is valid. The reason is that dishonesty soon becomes habitual; indeed it is the easiest of all immoral habits to acquire. Then the mind ceases to be able to distinguish clearly between truth and falsehood. Moreover one act of guile frequently needs to be upheld by another, so guile rapidly becomes a web which traps the soul. Even if the immediate consequences of honesty may be hurtful or uncomfortable, the long-term consequences of dishonesty are far worse.

To a mature Christian

61

The person who does no evil, yet also does no good,
cannot be considered good. There are many such people.
They fear being criticized or judged, so they are adept at
doing nothing that would provoke criticism or judgement. Perhaps also they have a strong sense of guilt; so
they avoid doing evil in order not to feel guilty. Yet their
hearts lack love and compassion for others. Thus they
have no desire to do good, and are quite unwilling to
make sacrifices for the sake of others. But these people
are even more miserable than those who devote
themselves wholly to evil. At least evil people enjoy some
momentary material pleasure from their actions. People
who do neither good nor evil enjoy neither material
pleasures nor the deeper spiritual joy which comes from
loving God and loving one's neighbour. They truly suffer
hell on earth. Their task is to rekindle the flame of love in
their hearts, by deliberately seeking to understand the
needs and feelings of others, and by discerning the same
needs and feelings within themselves.

To a mature Christian

There are some who call themselves Christian, and who attend worship regularly, yet perform no Christian actions in their daily lives. There are others who do not call themselves Christian, and who never attend worship, yet perform many Christian actions in their daily lives. Which of these two groups are the better disciples of Christ? Some would say that believing in Christ and worshipping him is what matters for salvation. But this is not what Jesus himself said. His teaching was almost entirely concerned with action, and with the motives which inspire action. He affirmed goodness of behaviour in whoever he found, whether the person was Jew or Roman, male or female. And he condemned those who kept all the religious requirements, yet were greedy and cruel. Jesus does not invite people to become his disciples for his own benefit, but to teach and guide them in the ways of goodness. And if a person can walk along that way without ever knowing the earthly Jesus, then we may say that he is following the spirit of Christ in his heart.

To a mature Christian

63

You may wonder how a person can worship God and proclaim Jesus as Lord, and yet not obey the commandments of Jesus. You may wonder how a person can open his arms in prayer and adoration, and yet have no desire to listen to God or even to his own conscience. Evil is like a fog which blinds people; so evil people can deceive themselves into believing that they are doing good. A rich man can oppress his servants and slaves, forcing them to work until every joint in their bodies aches and giving them the most meagre rations, and yet pride himself on his firm Christian discipline. A man caught up in a legal dispute may lie in court, causing an innocent man to be sent to gaol and bound in chains, and then thank God that he himself remains free. Such people are trying to make God a partner in their crime; and in the fog of evil they genuinely believe that God approves of their actions. If you wish to persuade an evil man to become good, you must lift that fog by means of patient and rational argument, so he can see the truth about himself.

To a mature Christian

64

You ask for a rule to govern your life. In making this request you show both anxiety and caution: anxiety because without a rule you fear you will stray from the way of Christ; caution because with a rule you believe you will be protected from moral danger. You are right to feel these emotions. God has given us freedom, so that at every moment of our lives we may choose good or evil. But in a single day we make so many diverse decisions that we cannot possibly weigh up the good and evil consequences of each decision. Thus we are liable to make foolish and wrong decisions that cause harm both to ourselves and to others. For this reason we need a rule. We need a simple set of moral principles that we can apply to each decision we have to make. This will not ensure that every decision is correct; at times the situation will be strange and unexpected, so the rule will be inadequate, or give the wrong guidance. But with a good rule our decisions will far more often be right than wrong.

To Celantia

65

You ask for a rule for a second reason. Jesus tells us that we should pray day by day and hour by hour to God, entrusting ourselves to his care, and seeking his guidance on our choices and decisions. At times we are eager to pray; we enjoy talking and listening to God, so we are very happy to devote large amounts of time to prayer. But at other times we find prayer dull and dry; we have no inclination to talk and listen to God, so we find all sorts of excuses not to pray. The most common excuse is lack of time — as if each day were so full that we could not find even a few moments to communicate with God. Yet such an excuse is plainly false: there is always time for prayer, even in the busiest day. Moreover, since God has supreme power over our lives, time spent communicating with him is of supreme value. To prevent ourselves making these excuses, we need a rule which compels us to pray each day, at a particular time, even when the heart is cold towards God.

To Celantia

If you are to have a rule to guide you, who is to write that rule? You ask me to do so, but I am not qualified. I cannot claim to be any wiser than you, so I could not presume to formulate any kind of law for you to follow. Should Jesus write your rule? The teaching of Jesus must be the primary guide for any disciple. Yet Jesus did not give clear rules. He gave us stories whose meaning is infinitely profound; and he gave us sermons in which every sentence and even every word is pregnant with truth. We cannot reduce these stories and sermons to a set of laws. The source for a rule is inside your own heart. What we call conscience is in fact a set of moral principles – a rule – which God himself has written. If you wish to formulate a rule you must listen to your conscience and discern these principles. Write down with you own hand on paper what God has written with his hand on the human heart.

To Celantia

67

I tell you that you should listen to your conscience; and you may reply by asking me how to listen. Conscience works by inducing feelings of guilt when you do wrong, and by inducing feelings of peace when you do right. So every day devote a few minutes to examining your conscience. Confess your sins by describing precisely, within you own mind, those actions which induced guilt during the previous day. Equally note carefully those actions which induced peace and tranquillity. After a few days you will discern similarities between guilt-inducing actions, and also similarities between actions that induce peace. From these similarities you can formulate general principles; and then you will have written your rule. You should then test your rule against the teaching of Jesus. If you have formulated principles which are contrary to his teaching, then you have misheard your conscience, and you must listen anew. But if your principles conform to his teaching, then you can be satisfied that your rule is correct.

To Celantia

God does not need us to obey him. He is perfect in himself; he needs nothing from outside himself in order to remain perfect. But we need his commands. His commands are more precious to us than the finest gold, and sweeter to us than honey. They are precious because without them we would be completely lost, not knowing how we should behave. They are sweet because only through obedience to God's commands can we know any joy, in this world and the next. Yet at times we treat God's laws as rusty bits of iron, fit only to be cast aside. And we think of them as sour and bitter, believing that the only sweetness in this life comes from satisfying our physical desires. If a man treats gold as iron, and regards honey as sour, we do not say that he is evil; we say he is blind and foolish. Equally when we treat God's commands with contempt, evil is the consequence; the cause is blindness and folly. To obey God's commands, we must first open our eyes to see how precious they are, and sharpen our wisdom to discern how sweet they are.

To Celantia

69

There are two kinds of divine command: one prohibits certain attitudes and actions; the other enjoins certain attitudes and actions. Thus, for example, hatred and malice are prohibited; love and generosity are enjoined. Some people regard the former kind of law as more important than the latter; they believe that if they avoid doing what God prohibits, that will be sufficient for them to be saved. Indeed many people have gained the impression that Christianity amounts to little more than a series of prohibitions. But in truth the second kind of law is equally important; indeed the first kind is useless without the second. A society in which people only avoided certain actions, but never did anything good, would be utterly dead; it would be like the valley of dry bones which the prophet describes. A society can only live if people love and serve one another. So when you are aware of hatred in your heart, do not simply suppress it, but transform it into love. When you desire to commit a malicious act, do not simply stop yourself; transform that act into a generous one.

To Celantia

70

All of us are influenced by the people among whom we live. We may imagine ourselves to be strong in heart and mind, able to withstand the influence of evil people. But if day by day we are living and working with evil people, their spirit gradually begins to affect our spirit; without realising it, we start to adopt their attitude and outlook, thinking and speaking as they do. Even drawing up a rule by which to live cannot protect us entirely from evil influence. So when you have composed your rule, and thus set yourself firmly on course for God's heavenly kingdom, you must also ensure that you live and work mainly among good people. Of course at times you must meet and talk to evil people, in order to try and influence them for good. After all, an evil person can only be converted to goodness by the influence of good people. But do not imagine that you are stronger than you really are. As you travel towards God's kingdom, you need loyal and loving companions by your side.

To Celantia

71

Look at the animals roaming the forest: God's spirit
dwells within them. Look at the birds flying across the
sky: God's spirit dwells within them. Look at the tiny
insects crawling in the grass: God's spirit dwells within
them. Look at the fish in the river and sea: God's spirit
dwells within them. There is no creature on earth in
whom God is absent. Travel across the ocean to the most
distant land, and you will find God's spirit in the
creatures there. Climb up the highest mountain, and you
will find God's spirit among the creatures who live at the
summit. When God pronounced that his creation was
good, it was not only that his hand had fashioned every
creature; it was that his breath had brought every creature
to life. Look too at the great trees of the forest; look at
the wild flowers and the grass in the fields; look even at
your crops. God's spirit is present within all plants as
well. The presence of God's spirit in all living beings is
what makes them beautiful; and if we look with God's
eyes, nothing on the earth is ugly.

To an elderly friend

72

When Jesus commands us to love our neighbours, he does not only mean our human neighbours; he means all the animals and birds, insects and plants, amongst whom we live. Just as we should not be cruel to other human beings, so we should not be cruel to any other species of creature. Just as we should love and cherish other human beings, so we should love and cherish all God's creation. We learn to love other humans by discerning their pleasure and pain, their joy and sorrow, and thence by sympathizing with them. We need only poke a horse with a sharp stick to discern the pain it can suffer; and when we stroke and slap that same horse on the neck, we can feel its pleasure. Thus we can love a horse in the same way as we can love another human being. Of course our love for other species is less full and less intense than our love for humans, because the range and the depth of their feelings are less than our own. Yet we should remember that all love comes from God; so when our love is directed towards an animal or even a tree, we are participating in the fullness of God's love.

To an elderly friend

73

Humankind is the pinnacle of God's creation. Human beings uniquely have the capacity to know the existence of their Creator, and to listen to his commands. And uniquely they possess freedom of choice, so they may obey his commands or disobey them. All other creatures are unaware of their Creator and act by instinct. This gives humankind superiority and power over other creatures. But this power can be used or abused. A person who is cruel to animals is abusing his power. A person who does not tend the wounds of the animals in his possession is abusing his power. A person who forces his donkeys and camels to carry loads beyond their capacity, so they groan under the weight, is abusing his power. But the person who takes pleasure in seeing animals healthy is using his power according to God's will. So is the person who heals his sick and wounded animals. Animals and plants provide food for us to eat; in return we should cherish those animals and plants.

To an elderly friend

74

When a person is young his mind and his body are active. And if he wishes to obey God's laws, he uses his energy to serve others, and so he can perform many good works. But as a person grows older his mind and his body become less active. Does this decline in energy mean that old people are less valuable, and can do less good, than young people? We should distinguish between active love and passive love. Active love does good through outward and visible movement; passive love does good through inward and invisible movement. The young person serves others with his mind and his body; the old person serves others with his soul. And the good works done in the person's youth are the perfect preparation for his old age. The young person is so active that he has little time for prayer; yet his good works are secretly strengthening his soul. Then in his later years, when his mind and body are less capable, his soul will radiate warm love both for God and for other people. Those who come close to such an old person receive that warmth and rejoice in it.

To an elderly friend

75

You have been a Christian for many years, as I have.
When we first became Christians we imagined that our
new faith was very complex. We thought that to be good
Christians we should have to learn much theology, and
to become well versed in philosophy. Now we have
learnt that Christianity is very simple. A good Christian is
one who prays regularly to God, seeking his guidance on
all matters; who never lies or curses; who loves all people,
friends and enemies alike; who does good even to those
who do evil to him; whose mind is free from malice;
who is always honest and never lies; and who regards
himself as superior to no one, but is humble towards
everyone. These precepts are very simple to understand,
and can be grasped by those with little intelligence. But
while they are simple to understand, they are hard to
follow. This too is something we have both discovered as
the years have passed. When we first became Christians
we thought that to behave like Christ would be easy.
Now we know otherwise; even after all these years we
still fall very far short of these simple standards.

To an elderly friend

76

The easiest sin to commit is to criticize a brother, calling him a fool. We are usually quite cautious about accusing a brother of an evil act, such as lying, stealing or adultery. We feel we must have ample evidence before making such an accusation. But to accuse a brother of doing something stupid or foolish hardly seems to matter. So we toss off such critical remarks quite lightly. Yet such criticism can hurt its victim very deeply. The words of criticism can stay in his head for days, weeks, months and even years after they were uttered – while the person who uttered them may forget them almost instantly. The reason is that most people feel little confidence in themselves and their abilities; far from being proud of their talents, they are unduly modest, and so undertake new tasks with great caution and even fear of failure. Thus critical remarks can destroy people's confidence completely, discouraging them to such a degree that they may never attempt the task that was criticized again. Therefore we must be far more vigilant against committing this easy sin than against many more obvious and greater sins.

To an elderly friend

Soon you and I will die. We do not know the day or the hour of death; God alone has such knowledge. But we can be certain that many more years have elapsed since birth than will pass between now and death. You say that you have no fear of death. I fear death because I fear having to account for my evil deeds before God. You say that you fear the process of dying. I do not fear dying because I know that God will not force me to suffer pain beyond my capacity to endure it. Elderly people like ourselves frequently make attempts to amend their behaviour, hoping that God will forgive past sins and judge them on present goodness. God will not be swayed by that kind of calculation. It is the heart, not the mind, that needs to change: we must learn to love God more fully. And love coming from the heart makes no calculation. If a person loves God with his whole heart, he will entrust himself to God's love, without seeking to sway God's judgement by displays of good behaviour. If my heart could change in such a way, my fear of death would disappear.

To an elderly friend

78

You have a deep desire to appear wise to others. Yet in
your heart you have no confidence in yourself: you do
not regard yourself as wise. So in the company of others
you remain silent; even when the conversation turns to
spiritual and religious matters, where words of wisdom
are most necessary, you remain silent. You hope that
people will interpret your silence as a sign of the depth of
your wisdom – so deep that mere words cannot communicate it. Some people try to deceive others with
dishonest words; you are trying to deceive others by
dishonest silence. If you possess wisdom on particular
matters, it is your duty under God to express this wisdom
to others, so they can benefit from it. If you do not
possess wisdom on matters of importance, it is your duty
under God to ask questions of those who do possess
wisdom, so you can learn from it. In either case you must
speak. This does not mean that words should flow
constantly from your mouth like a river. Use words
sparingly, so that they express precisely what you mean.
But without words you will remain ignorant and stupid.

To a young friend

79

The fact that you want to appear wise to others assures me that you understand the nature and importance of wisdom. There are many foolish people who do not think that wisdom matters: they scorn and laugh at those who possess it. The first step from folly to wisdom is to recognize your own folly, and to perceive the value of wisdom. You have made this first step. The next step is to seek the company of wise people and to listen to them. Do not be afraid of revealing your ignorance to a wise person. Wisdom confers on a person humility; so a wise person will never rebuke or despise an ignorant person. On the contrary when you confess your ignorance openly to a wise person, he will love and cherish you as a father loves and cherishes a son. For a father the greatest pleasure is to teach his son; for a wise man the greatest pleasure is to dispel ignorance. Do not be afraid also of asking questions of a wise person, however stupid those questions may seem. Wisdom confers on a person patience; so a wise person will happily respond to the simplest question, if it is asked in a sincere desire to learn the truth.

To a young friend

Wisdom carries a price: full knowledge of your own sins. Imagine an ignorant and foolish man standing before God's court of judgement. His sins are read out to him, but he is utterly bewildered, because he was not aware of the difference between right and wrong, good and evil. And imagine a wise man standing before God's court. When his sins are read out, he is filled with anguish and cries out for mercy, because he knew well the difference between right and wrong, good and evil. Even on earth the foolish man is free of guilt, because his ignorance about sin leaves his conscience dormant; but the wise man is wracked with guilt at every sin he commits. So it may be wise to remain ignorant! Yet the price of wisdom is far, far less than its reward. Just as the wise man understands sin, he also understands the joy and the peace which come from leading a good and holy life. This joy and peace are beyond the reach of the ignorant and the foolish; they can only be obtained through acquiring wisdom.

To a young friend

81

In what does wisdom consist? Does it consist in grasping the wild speculations of philosophers? No, because these speculations fill the mind, but do not touch the soul. Does it consist in clever rhetoric and elegant phrases? No, because words which sparkle on the surface are usually rotten beneath. Does a person need to be intelligent and well educated to be wise? No, because the greatest wisdom is often found amongst those who cannot even read. Wisdom consists in listening to the commandments of God, and obeying them. A person who has heard that God commands people to be generous, and then shares what he has with the poor, is truly wise. A person who has heard that God commands people to love their enemies, and then performs acts of charity towards those who hate him, is truly wise. A person who has heard that God commands people to repent of their sins, and then confesses his sins to his victims and makes good the harm he has done, is truly wise. A person who has heard that God commands people to forgive the sins of others, and then reaches out in love to his persecutors, is truly wise.

To a young friend

82

To be wise is to act wisely. There is no wisdom that does not express itself in action. When a young person like you first aspires to wisdom, he may imagine that wisdom is the route to a tranquil and even comfortable life. He may see himself in years to come dispensing words of advice and solace to others, and receiving effusive words of gratitude. Certainly wise people do enjoy the privilege of serving others in this way. But there is no outward tranquillity for the wise man, and probably little physical comfort. Wisdom confers on a person the gift of discernment: he can see clearly the needs of others. Wisdom also confers the virtue of zeal: when he sees the needs of others, he cannot rest until he has satisfied them. So a wise person is also a busy person, to the limits of his strength. Yet the lack of outward rewards is more than compensated by inner rewards. The wise person may not enjoy outward tranquillity, but his heart and soul are at peace. He may not enjoy physical comfort, but his heart and soul are filled with divine joy.

To a young friend

83

The law of God, which Christ preached, is summarized in the command to love: Christ commands us to love God, and to love our neighbours as ourselves. Applying this command to the choices and decisions that are made every day, and every hour of every day, means following a simple rule: a person should only do to others what he would want them to do to himself; and he should not do to others what he would not want them to do to him. Sometimes this rule needs to be modified. Each person is different, with different needs: so it may be right occasionally to help another person in a way that you would not wish to be helped yourself. Yet in general the rule shows the way towards happiness, justice and peace. Imagine the world if everyone lived according to this rule. There would be no rich and poor, but all would be equal in wealth. There would be no wars, because no one could conceive of attacking and killing another person. There would be no fear, but instead each person would regard all his neighbours as friends. God's kingdom would have come to earth, as it is in heaven.

To a young friend

84

Old people often envy the young. They envy the vigour and good health of the young. They envy the greater capacity which young people possess for physical pleasure and enjoyment. They envy the years which young people have ahead of them on earth. In truth the young should envy the old. While old people have less physical and mental vigour, they have greater spiritual vigour. While they have fewer material pleasures, they have greater capacity for spiritual joy. The old are thus better prepared for death, and thence for life beyond death; so the fewer years lying ahead of them should be a cause for celebration not self-pity. Yet while a young person like yourself may imagine that you have many years ahead, you cannot be certain. The soul is attached to the body by a fragile thread which may snap at any moment. Thus although you are younger than I am, you may die before me. Therefore you should not merely envy old age, but you should also imitate its qualities. Divert your mental and physical vigour into spiritual things; and let spiritual things become your major source of pleasure. In this way you will be ready for death whenever it occurs.

To a young friend

FORTHCOMING TITLES

THE LITTLE GIDDING PRAYER BOOK

The new edition will contain a pattern of daily, weekly and annual worship for individuals and groups. It will be very easy to use, with a cycle of New Testament readings, and psalms drawn from throughout the Old Testament, printed within. It also provides a context, within daily prayer, to use the books of non-biblical readings which are published each quarter – see below.

THE FIRST MARTYRS
Their Defences and Testimonies

When tried by the Roman authorities, men like Justin, Athenagoras and Polycarp – Christian leaders in the second century – gave brilliant defences of their faith. They also wrote letters from prison which are deeply moving. This book provides an edited and accessible version of these writings.

THE LOST EPISTLES
Advice from the Early Church

Throughout the second century, epistles from great leaders were passed eagerly from church to church. Some of these epistles were eventually included in the canon of scripture, and have been studied by Christians ever since. Others, which had no direct connection with the apostles, were left out; and were soon virtually forgotten except by scholars. Yet they contain wisdom and insight which in places is equal to that of Paul, Peter, James and the rest. This popular edition brings these lost epistles, by such men as Clement and Ignatius, to the general reader.

JOHN CASSIAN
East Meets West
Trained as a monk in the Egyptian desert, John Cassian travelled to western Europe at the time when Rome fell. He founded monasteries in France, which in turn profoundly influenced the Celtic church in Britain and Ireland. His writings call ordinary men and women to the primitive simplicity of the gospel.

EUSEBIUS
The First Christian Historian
Much of our knowledge of the early church comes from the pen of Eusebius, who was an intimate friend of Emperor Constantine early in the fourth century. The stories he relates vibrate with spiritual passion – which at times leads to great heroism, and at times pitches the church into terrible disputes.

JOHN CHRYSOSTOM
The Spirit of Protest
Growing up in the late fourth century when the bishops and clergy were becoming corrupted by wealth and power, John Chrysostom was angered by the gap between church and gospel. He believed that Christians were called to live simply and to serve the poor and the sick – and if necessary take political action in the cause of justice. By popular demand he became Patriarch of Constantinople, but was later driven into exile by his powerful enemies. His sermons are masterpieces of both spiritual and political oratory.